BIBLE GAMES

EDITH BEAVERS ALLEN

*Dedicated to
my family
and members of the
Calvary Baptist Church
Clearwater, Florida*

FOREWORD

There is no better way to increase one's knowledge of anything than by doing.

These games are designed to help young people and adults become more familiar with New Testament teachings. They are quite entertaining as well as instructive.

CONTENTS

GREETING GAMES

SCRABBLE GAMES

IDENTIFICATION GAMES

SPACE GAMES

CONVERSATION GAMES

READ GAMES

NAME GAMES

ACTIVE GAMES

CONTEST GAMES

RELAY GAMES

ONE WORD GAMES

Greeting Games

HOWDY DOODY

Howdy Doody is a get acquainted game. Leader will need to get several Bible pictures that are not too large. One picture for two guests. Cut pictures in half and as guests arrive give each a half. Leader should have a helper to assist. Leader may keep one part of each picture and give the other part to his helper. Leader will give a half to each girl and helper will give a part to each boy upon arrival. When all guests are assembled, leader will explain that the girls must find the boy with the matching half of her picture. They must say, "Howdy Doody, my name is Mary," or whatever their name happens to be and continue in conversation for at least two minutes. Perhaps leader will request that they be partners for the evening. Pictures may be found from someone who works in the Sunday school department.

NAME IS THE GAME

As guests arrive leader gives each a pencil and paper. When all are assembled, leader tells them that they are to circulate among each other and ask guests their name and write down as many names as they can find that are found in the New Testament. Even though a guest might know another's first and last name, the middle name also counts and the player would certainly want to add this name to his list if it were found in the New Testament. Example: A guest's first name might be Marjorie which could not be used, but Marjorie's middle name might be Elizabeth which could be used. The guest getting the most names in a given time is the winner and may be given a prize. Names may be counted twice or more if there are two or more guests having the same name.

Some names found in the New Testament:

11

James	Joseph or Joe	Anna
John	David	Julia
Philip	Thomas or Tom	Claudia
Paul	Alexander or Alex	Eunice
Peter	Elizabeth	Hannah
Andrew	Mary	Janna or Jane
Stephen	Martha	Phebe
Lucas	Dorcas	Rachel
Jason	Lydia	Rhoda
Marcus or Mark	Priscilla	Rufus
Nicolas or Nick	Sarah	
Timothy or Tim		

BLIND DATE

Write or print a Scripture verse on strips of paper. Give one to each girl and have her tear it in half. Ask her to tie one part in her handkerchief and keep the other. When all have done this, place handkerchiefs on a table at the far end of the room. When the leader blows the whistle, the boys must run to the table and select a hankie. He must untie the hankie, take out the Scripture verse and find the girl who has the other part, thereby finding his date for the evening.

TITLE INTRODUCTION

Leader should prepare in advance slips of paper on which are written titles of hymns. There may be one or more on each paper. Leader will need a helper to stand with him near the door as guests arrive. As guests enter pin a paper on the skirt of the girl's dress and one on each cuff of the boy's trousers. When all guests have arrived, leader should give each a piece of paper and pencil and have guests list as many titles as they can find on the garments of other guests. Naturally as guests mingle about they will also want to keep others from reading the names on their papers; however, they must not conceal papers with their hands. After a certain time, the leader stops the game and checks the list of each guest, giving a prize to the one getting the most titles. Leader should keep a list of titles used. Titles may be found in the index of a hymnbook.

TRADE NAME

Leader will need to have available the following: An empty medicine bottle bearing a label, a small plastic box containing a fishhook, a book pertaining to law, a toy pistol, a Bible, a silver bracelet, a small hammer, an empty box on which is inscribed *tax* and a piece of leather. Leader should also prepare in advance cards on which is written the name of a character mentioned in the New Testament, engaged in various trades representing items mentioned. For example: The medicine bottle represents Luke, the physician. Each name of a person used must be represented by some such items. Names suggested are to be used with the things mentioned.

Peter — fisherman (fishhook)
Gamaliel — a lawyer (book of law)
Paulus — deputy (toy gun)
Philip — evangelist (Bible)
Demetrius — silversmith (bracelet)
Joseph — carpenter (hammer)
Matthew — tax collector (box labled *tax*)
Simon — tanner (piece of leather)

As guests arrive, leader will need to have an assistant stand with him near the door. Pin a card on each boy and give each girl any one of the items used. When all have arrived, have the boys introduce themselves by finding the girl with the item which represents his trade.

FIND A PARTNER

As the girls arrive, leader pins on the front of each a small card on which is written the name of a book in the New Testament. Leader pins on each boy a Scripture verse selected from one of these books. When all the guests are assembled, leader explains to guests that each must find a partner by matching verses and names of books in which they are found.

WHAT A BIRD

Before guests arrive the leader should have prepared some small cards on which is written the name of a bird mentioned in the Bible. One card for each guest. Using bobby pins, pin a card on top of the head of each guest upon arrival. When all have assembled, give each guest paper and pencil and explain that they are to mingle, find and list as many different kinds of birds as they can. Players must not remove cards until the game is over. A prize is given to the player who has the largest number listed in a given time. A list of birds is as follows: eagle, hawk, hen, dove, cuckoo, crane, swan, swallow, raven, sparrow, stork, pelican, heron, kite, night hawk, ostrich, partridge, peacock, pigeon, turtle dove, quail, screech owl, little owl, horned owl, great owl and vulture.

Scrabble Games

UNUSUAL FACTS OF THE BIBLE

Give guests copies of the following sentences and have them untangle the word to complete the fact. Omit answers in parenthesis.

1. Young widows are prone to *sospig*. (gossip)
2. A king was eaten of *morws*. (worms)
3. A law suit is not to be defended by *aniristchs*. (Christians)
4. In I Peter Satan is compared to a *niol*. (lion)
5. *Zalsaur* was raised from the dead. (Lazarus)
6. *Pahecs* was another name for Peter. (Cephas)
7. A *teag* opened of itself. (Gate)
8. *Orehd* had a birthday party. (Herod)
9. *Rodasc* was a dressmaker. (Dorcas)
10. *Hahtita* was another name for Dorcas. (Tabitha)
11. *Tasree* is mentioned only once in the Bible. (Easter)
12. *Uersile* is used only once in the Bible. (leisure)

BUILDER UP'ERS

Draw pictures of boys and girls approximately seven inches in length and two or three inches wide. Make one for each guest. Color each leaving the bodies white on which print the following for guests to unscramble. Explain to them that the words are character builders and Christian qualities.

Answers are in parenthesis:

1. Teguairtd (gratitude)
2. Petneeamcr (temperance)
3. Somaspcoin (compassion)
4. Tenapiec (patience)
5. Dseiknns (kindness)
6. Tnoabmii (ambition)
7. Felhessnssiun (unselfishness)
8. Ydnlerif (friendly)
9. Iayhtcr (charity)
10. Tahif (faith)
11. Ylolyta (loyalty)
12. Oyj (joy)
13. Syohetn (honesty)
14. Smdtoe (modest)
15. Ryupti (purity)
16. Tnonetc (content)

JUMBLED PARABLES

The leader should prepare copies of the following for each guest. Guests are allowed only fifteen minutes to untangle the parables. The guest who gets the most correct may be given a prize. A picture puzzle would be a suitable prize.

Here are some you may want to use: Others may be found listed under Parables in the specialized index of the Bible. Answers are in parenthesis.

1. Het toem dan mabe (The mote and beam)
2. Eht renrab igf reet (The barren fig tree)
3. Hawet dna raset (Wheat and tares)
4. Hte sartdum dsee (The mustard seed)
5. Teh gliaoprd osn (The prodigal son)
6. Het speeh nad eht agsot (The sheep and the goats)
7. Eth ent natlest (The ten talents)
8. Teh ieesraph dan bialncup (The Pharisee and publican)
9. Aeveln diednh ni amel (Leaven hidden in meal)
10. Arpel fo aretg ciepr (Pearl of great price)
11. Eth adrg etn (The drag net)
12. Ihcr amn nad Suazarl (Rich man and Lazarus)

AN EAR HAS LOST ITS SENSE

Give the ear back its sense by changing the first letter of each word to fit the word to the correct definition. Copies of words and definitions may be given each guest.

Example: Answer to number one is (d) making the word *dear* to fit the proper definition: a polite address. Game is merely an exchange of first letters.

		Answers	
1. N ear — a polite address.		1. (d) dear
2. H ear — to pull apart.		2. (t) tear
3. Y ear — a clumsy mammal.		3. (b) bear
4. B ear — a feeling of uneasiness.		4. (f) fear
5. T ear — a period that passes.		5. (y) year
6. R ear — to clothe.		6. (w) wear

7. P ear — to drop from the eye.
8. F ear — to become worn.
9. T ear — to listen to.
10. D ear — a fruit.
11. W ear — a mechanism performing a specific function.
12. W ear — to scorch lightly
13. L ear — close in relationship.
14. S ear — an English humorist and painter.
15. G ear — the back part of something.

7. (t) tear
8. (w) wear
9. (h) hear
10. (p) pear
11. (g) gear
12. (s) sear
13. (n) near
14. (L) Lear-Edward
15. (r) rear

UNRAVEL AND MATCH

1. Lhpipi
2. Erpet
3. Thwamet
4. Racods
5. Msnio
6. Lapsuu
7. Daily
8. Qaluai
9. Lsieurcon
10. Rapgiap

fisherman
evangelist
tax collector
saleslady
centurion
king
seamstress
tanner
deputy
tentmaker

Answers

1. Philip — the evangelist
2. Peter — fisherman
3. Matthew — tax collector
4. Dorcas — seamstress
5. Simon — a tanner

6. Paulus — a deputy
7. Lydia — a saleslady
8. Aquila — tentmaker
9. Cornelius — a centurion
10. Agrippa — a king

THINGS SCRAMBLED

Things scrambled are related to the parable of the Prodigal Son.

1. Otrpnoi
2. Amfnie
3. Iensw
4. Ukhss

Portion (of goods)
Famine
Swine
Husks

5. Ervsnats	Servants
6. Rebda	Bread
7. Athref	Father
8. Noisspacmo	Compassion
9. Kcen	Neck
10. Oebr	Robe
11. Girn	Ring
12. Hosse	Shoes
13. Acfl	Calf
14. Oslt	Lost
15. Oufdn	Found
16. Andginc	Dancing
17. Rotbreh	Brother
18. Rifdens	Friends

IT'S A BACKWARD WORD

Can you find the backword word?

The words listed, spelled backwards, fit one of the following definitions. Leader should prepare copies and lists of words in advance. Supply guests with pencil and allow them five minutes to match the word to the correct definition.

Words are: none, mane, tang, loop, draw, net, rats, tips, live, tip, lived and peels.

Definitions		Answers:	
1.	A hollow in the earth	1.	pit
2.	A place east of Jordan	2.	Enon
3.	A small insect	3.	gnat
4.	A number	4.	ten
5.	A reservoir	5.	pool
6.	A heavenly body	6.	star
7.	A city in Judah	7.	Enam
8.	To guard	8.	ward
9.	Wickedness	9.	evil
10.	Demon	10.	devil
11.	To slumber	11.	sleep
12.	To eject saliva	12.	spit

TOPSY-TURVY

Write or type the following topsy-turvy words on paper, a copy for each guest. Let each write the word correctly. Words are names of places mentioned in the New Testament. Leader should set a time limit and give a prize to the one who gets the most correct and a consolation prize to the guest getting the least number.

1. Ianacemdo
2. Viadd
3. Elegila
4. Anezarht
5. Raysi
6. Mejalusre
7. Thorcin
8. Sahtne
9. Hcanoit
10. Temehhleb
11. Eorm
12. Nojdar
13. Rmcnaepau
14. Hesupes
15. Olsoesc

1. Macedonia
2. David (city of)
3. Galilee
4. Nazareth
5. Syria
6. Jerusalem
7. Corinth
8. Athens
9. Antioch
10. Bethlehem
11. Rome
12. Jordan
13. Capernaum
14. Ephesus
15. Colosse

IDENTIFICATION GAMES

MY GIFT REPRESENTS

Each guest is asked to bring an inexpensive gift, not to exceed a certain amount. The gift must represent something in the Scripture. For example: Guest might bring a candle which would represent Matthew 5:5, "Neither do men light a candle, and put it under a bushel but on a candlestick; and it giveth light unto all that are in the house." A candle holder or a flashlight might also represent this verse. Guests might bring something gold which would represent a gift to the baby Jesus. Gifts should be wrapped. As the guest enters, gifts are dropped into a large box which has been placed near the door. At a designated time the leader or hostess places the box in the center of the room and each guest must come forward and pick up the first package he touches as he reaches in the box. If a guests selects his own package he may choose another. When all gifts have been taken, they are opened and the leader asks each person to describe what his gift seems to represent. Whether his guess is right or not he may keep the gift providing the giver will identify himself and tell what he intended his gift to represent. There are many things that could bring a good laugh and also be useful, such as a cooking utensil (vessel) or a box of salt, etc.

HIDDEN HYMNS

Give each player a copy of the following story which has been prepared in advance, minus copy in parenthesis of the words which indicates the answers. Within a certain time limit set by the leader, each player is to find the titles of the fourteen hymns hidden in the sentences. A prize may be given to the player who finishes first. A tiny hymnbook would be suitable as a prize.

The (Bible) is a (divine) and (holy book). If we (only believe) in its word and (trust and obey), (what a friend we) will (have in Jesus). If we (take time) from our busy life (to be holy) and do (our best) to stay on (higher ground), he will (draw near) to us.

He was (*nailed to the cross*) and (*he died of a broken heart*) but (*some sweet day*) there will be a (*gathering home*) and (*rest for the weary*) (*safe in the arms of Jesus*).

Answers are:
Holy Bible, Book Divine — Only Believe — Trust and Obey — What a Friend We Have in Jesus — Take Time to Be Holy — Our Best — Higher Ground — Draw near — Nailed to the Cross — He Died of a Broken Heart — Some Sweet Day — Gathering Home — Rest For the Weary — Safe in the Arms of Jesus.

NAME THE ART OF THE CRAFTSMAN

Listed below are some craftsmen mentioned in the New Testament. Can you identify their craft?

1. Demetrius was a .... (silversmith)
2. Alexander was a .... (coppersmith or brazier)
3. Jesus was a .... (carpenter)
4. Simon was a .... (tanner)
5. Aquila was a .... (tentmaker)
6. Priscilla was a .... (tentmaker)
7. Paul was a .... (tentmaker)
8. Joseph was a .... (carpenter)
9. Dorcas was a .... (dressmaker)
10. Tabitha was a .... (dressmaker)

WHAT GROWS IN YOUR GARDEN

Get a tiny piece of as many kinds of vegetables (mentioned in the Bible) as possible and put them in a small bowl. Keep a record of the things used. Give each guest a pencil and paper and have them write down as many things as they can remember when the bowl has passed to all players. The bowl must not remain in a player's hand but may be passed rather slowly and players must not start to write until all players have been handed the bowl. Player who guesses the largest number of things is given a prize. An appropriate prize would be a garden tool.

Examples of things to use:

A piece of *melon*, a *candy mint*, a piece of *mustard greens*, *garlic*, *grape*, grain of *corn*, piece of *citron*, a sprinkle of *cinnamon*, piece of *cucumber*, an *olive*, piece of *onion*, sprinkle of *salt*, blade of *grass*, a *husk* from *corn*, a *nut*, a *bean*, a piece of *apple*, a sprig of *hay*, a *fig*, and a slice of *green pepper*.

COUNTDOWN

Questions should be typed for each guest. When folded papers and pencils have been given out, the leader starts the countdown as players answer questions. He must count aloud starting at twenty and when he has reached number one, players put down their pencils. Leader may count as fast as he wishes. Player who gets the most correct answers is declared the winner.

Answers

20. Who is the third person of the Trinity?

(Holy Spirit)

19. What is a word meaning a symbol of "the last"?

(omega)

18. Name the small island where Paul was shipwrecked?

(Melita)

17. What is rising of the body from death called?

(resurrection)

16. What was a robe called that was made of coarse material resembling a sack and held by a matching girdle?

(sackcloth)

15. Name the wife of Zebedee, mother of James and John.

(Salome)

14. What is a tithe?

(tenth)

13. Name a sect of Judaism in the time of Christ.

(Pharisees)

12. What was the interest for money or loans called?

(usury)

11. What is another name for the Sea of Gennesaret?

(Sea of Galilee)

10. What is a well-known word among Christians which means truth or so be it?

(Amen)

9. What was a feeding place for animals known as?

(manger)

8. What is another name for Matthew?

(Levi)

7. How many Mary's are mentioned in the New Testament?

(six)

6. What was an ingredient in the holy ointment also used as a perfume? A gift of it was brought to Jesus.

(myrrh)

5. What is a short story used as comparison called?

(parable)

4. What is meant by the word straightway?

(at once)

3. What is a sepulchre?

(burial place)

2. Who was the first Christian martyr?

(Stephen)

1. What is a saint?

(Title of a Christian)

Your Countdown Score

Twenty correct answers is a Blast Off 50 points. Man in space
Fifteen correct answers is a Hold 20 points. 10 min.
Ten correct answers is a Hold 15 points. 30 min.
Five correct answers 5 points. Postponement
No correct answers No score. Failure

QUALITY CHART

The leader should prepare in advance a Quality Chart for each guest. The Quality Chart is simply a piece of 8x4 cardboard, colored around the edge, on which is written the words below. Leader tells guests that everyone is diet conscious and worries about eating the right kind of food. He explains that Christians are diet conscious too, but also body builders in another sense as to qualities. Leader tells players that both good and bad qualities are listed on his chart and each is to select the good qualities and those which Christians should avoid. A green and red crayon may be given to each player, underlining the good qualities in green and the bad ones in red.

Words are:

1. Vacillation
2. Sanguineous
3. Reliance
4. Emulous
5. Mundanus
6. Temerity
7. Probity
8. Benevolence
9. Commiserate
10. Diffidence
11. Contumelious
12. Supererogate
13. Obsequious
14. Supercilious
15. Anarchism
16. Abstemious
17. Unremitting
18. Dilatoriness
19. Diabolism
20. Placability

Good Qualities:

Reliance — is trust
Unremitting — not stopping
Abstemious — abstaining from alcoholic liquor
Benevolence — good and kind
Obsequious — devoted or dutiful
Sanguineous — confident, hope
Probity — honesty
Commiserate — to sympathize or condole
Supererogate — to do more than is required
Placability — forgiving

Bad Qualities:

Vacillation — indecision or wavering mind
Diffidence — lack of confidence
Emulous — envious or jealous
Dilatoriness — quality of being late or tardiness
Contumelious — insulting
Diabolism — dealing with witchcraft or belief of such
Mundanus — worldly
Temerity — reckless or rashness
Supercilious — pride
Anarchism — resistance to organized government or lawless

MIRACLE OR PARABLE

Prepare in advance (written or typed) copies of the following references. Let each guest identify them as to those which refer to the parables of Christ and the ones that relate to the miracles of Christ.

1.	Tares	1.	parable
2.	Calms the tempest	2.	miracle
3.	Feeds five thousand	3.	miracle
4.	Grain of mustard seed	4.	parable
5.	Blasts the fig tree	5.	miracle
6.	Precious pearl	6.	parable
7.	Prodigal Son	7.	parable
8.	Restores daughter of Jairus	8.	miracle
9.	Laborers in the vineyard	9.	parable
10.	The virgins	10.	parable
11.	A draught of fishes	11.	miracle
12.	Talents	12.	parable

THE VEGETABLE KINGDOM

Can you identify the following?

1.	Sycamore	1.	a bushy tree
2.	Spelt	2.	wheat
3.	Mandrake	3.	a narcotic plant
4.	Calamus	4.	spice
5.	Carob	5.	a tree
6.	Darnel	6.	weed
7.	Tares	7.	weeds
8.	Flag	8.	water plants
9.	Millet	9.	grass
10.	Pomegranate	10.	tree with red flowers
11.	Terebinth	11.	small tree
12.	Spikenard	12.	a plant

Space Games

A WORD THAT PURRS

Fill in the blank spaces in each Scripture verse with a word that purrs. The correct word begins with *per*. All are sayings of Paul. Leader may make copies for guests in advance.

1. "In journeying often, in................of water, in............... of robbers, in....................by mine own countrymen, in ....by the heathen, in....................in the city, in ....in the wilderness, in....................in the sea, in ....among false brethren." (*perils*)
2. To Barjesus, "Will thou not cease to....................the right ways of the Lord?" (*pervert*)
3. "I glory through Jesus Christ in things which.................... to God." (*pertain*)
4. "For your sakes forgave I it in the....................of Christ." (*person*)
5. "I take pleasure in....................for Christ's sake." (*persecution*)
6. "Though our outward man................yet the inward man is renewed day by day." (*perish*)
7. "....................disputings of men of corrupt minds, and destitute of the truth, supposing that gain is godliness." (*perverse*)
8. "But they that will be rich fall into temptation and a snarl, and into many foolish and hurtful lusts, which drown men in destruction and ...." (*perdition*)
9. "But I trust to tarry awhile with you, if the Lord...................." (*permit*)
10. "Make you....................in every good work to do His will." (*perfect*)

FILL IN SENTENCES

Explain to the players that the following sentences may be completed with words made up of combinations with the word, "over." Leader may make copies of sentences for guests in advance.

1. "And take heed to yourselves, lest at any time your hearts be................with surfeiting, and drunkenness, and cares of this life, and so that day come upon you unawares!" (overcharged)
2. "I have................the world." (overcome)
3. "Which had the golden censer, and the ark of the covenant................round about with gold." (overlaid)
4. "So that contrariwise you ought rather to forgive him, and comfort him, lest perhaps such a one should be swallowed up with................sorrow." (overmuch)
5. "The Holy Ghost hath made you................, to feed the church of God." (overseers)
6. "While he yet spake, behold, a bright cloud................ them." (overshadowed)
7. "Feed the flock of God which is among you, taking the ....thereof, not by constraint, but willingly." (oversight)
8. "Who concerning the truth have erred, saying that the resurrection is past already; and ....the faith of some." (overthrow)
9. "And Jesus................the tables of the money changers, and the seats of them that sold doves." (overthrew)
10. "Go into the village................you, and straightway ye shall find an ass tied, and a colt with her; loose them, and bring them unto me." (over against)

IN IS OUT — IN IS IN

Explain to players that only the first part of a word is in the following quotations. Where the word *in* appears with an underlined space, players are to complete the word making a correct quotation. Written copies of the sentences should be prepared in advance.

1. "I ask therefore for what in............ ye have sent for me?" (*intent*)
2. "For I delight in the law of God after the in................ man." (*inward*)
3. "Now unto the King eternal, immortal, in................ the only wise God." (*invisible*)

4. "Because there was no room for them in the in....." (*inn*)
5. "And because in.............shall abound, the love of many shall wax cold." (*iniquity*)
6. "I would not write with paper and in....." (*ink*)
7. "I am in........... of the blood of this just person." (*innocent*)
8. "In all things I am in............... both to be full and to be hungry." (*instructed*)
9. "All scripture is given by in.................... of God." (*inspiration*)
10. "Likewise the Spirit also helpeth our in........................." (*infirmities*)
11. "The spirit itself maketh in.................... for us with groanings which cannot be uttered." (*intercession*)
12. "Neither yield ye your members as in.................... of unrighteousness unto sin." (*instruments*)
13. "To an in.................... in...................., and undefiled, and that fadeth not away, reserved in heaven for you." (*inheritance*) (*incorruptible*)
14. "Therefore thou art in...................., O man, whosoever thou art that judgest." (*inexcusable*)
15. "The Lord is risen in.........., and hath appeared to Simon." (*indeed*)
16. "The same shall drink of the wine, of the wrath of God, which is poured out without mixture into the cup of his in................." (*indignation*)

THE ROMANCE OF E, N AND X

Love or charity is the life of a Christian. What book could be complete without a love story? Let couples work together on this game. Give each couple a paper on which has been typewritten the romance of E. N, and X. Leader should leave out words which have been italicized. Be sure to underline a blank space where the word is to be filled in. Leader may explain to players that the correct answer must begin with an *E*. Also, that the missing word will be a word with the emphasis on a certain letter which is found preceding each blank space. Example: Poor E was silent after she and N became .... The letter *N* gives a clue to *en*gaged where the emphasis is on the N in this particular word, in its pronunciation. Give a prize to the couple getting the most correct words. If leader wishes to simplify the game, he may give couples a list of the missing words written in jumbled fashion on the back of the papers on which the story is written.

Poor E was silent after she and N became *engaged*. E had thought that she and N would *enjoy* life. But N was full of *envy* and every man who looked at E became N's *enemy*. E talked to N and tried to *enlighten* him but it looked as though the romance of E and N would *end*.

One day N *entertained* for E, and E met X. X didn't *exclude* E from everything. Though E remained silent X took over. X regarded E with high *esteem*. The *estate* of E was soon to change. X said there was no *excuse* for any man to *exercise* jealousy to such *excess*. E soon found X to be the *extreme* opposite of N. X was a shining *example* and more than any girl could *expect*. E learned from X how to *express* herself and E found a way to *escape* from N. E and X *examined* the whole *experience* and E found X to be an *expert*. E wanted X in *exchange* for N. E learned from X *exactly* what she must do. E and X began to *execute* the plan. E prepared a dinner *especially* for N. N *enquired* of E about this *event*. For now N knew that E was more his *equal* since E had left N and *entered* into a friendship with X. E soon *established* this by telling N that she could *endure* him no longer. E informed N that she did not wish to *enjoin* him as his *espousal*. Then E was accused by N of *enticing* X. But this time E could see *evil* and E *estranged* herself from N. N realized that E had really had *enough* of him. But because of this trouble N became an *ensample* to others. Now E knew that N was not *endowed* with quality. So E went to X and *extended* her arms. X would always *exceed* N. X was *exalted* and nothing could *excel* the joy of X. X and E at last found *eternal* happiness.

ADD THE REMAINDER

Add the remainder of the word to the letter underlined in each of the following sentences. Words are all found in the New Testament.

1. One who eats to excess is a g............ . (glutton)
2. A broken piece is a f................ . (fragment)
3. Women should wear the o............... of a quiet spirit instead of jewels. (ornament)
4. A very fragrant resin imported from Arabia and used for perfume is f....................... . (frankincense)
5. An insect sent as a plague but also used for food is a l................ . (locust)
6. The top piece of a door frame that rests on two side posts is called a l............ . (lintel)
7. A man engaged in the making of earthenware was called a p............ . (potter)
8. The term applied to one who rejects the teachings of Christ is u.................... . (unbeliever)
9. A keeper of a prison who tortured a prisoner was known as a t.................... . (tormentor)
10. A snake is called a s................ . (serpent)
11. A word which signifies religious and political parties of the Jews is s........ . (sect)
12. A people named from their chief city Rome are the R................ . (Romans)
13. Foretelling of events by divine revelation is called p............. . (prophecy)

INTRODUCE A LETTER

Introduce a letter to a certain word in each of the following sentences to make a correct statement. Leader may prepare copies for guests in advance. Omit italicizing of the words and the answers given in parenthesis. The answer is always a first letter in a word. Give a prize to the one getting the largest number correct.

1. Paul gave testimony of God's *race*. (g) grace
2. Do not cast *earls* before swine. (p) pearls
3. He went into the *orders* of Tyre and Sidon. (b) borders
4. When the *ranch* puts forth leaves, summer is near. (b) branch

5. Jesus said, "O fools, and *low* of heart to believe." (s) slow
6. Peter said, "Thou art in *all* of bitterness." (g) gall
7. Philip, the evangelist, had *our* daughters. (f) four
8. Cornelius said, "A man stood before me in *right* clothing." (b) bright
9. Under the old law we were *hut* up into the faith. (s) shut
10. *Ark* is one of the books in the New Testament. (M) Mark
11. The Word of God is sharper than any two-edged *word*. (s) sword
12. They did not glorify God when they *new* Him. (k) knew
13. His head and hair were white as *now*. (s) snow
14. He is a living precious *tone*. (S) Stone
15. The Lord is not *lack* concerning His promise. (s) slack
16. A meek spirit is of great *rice* in the sight of God. (p) price
17. In the days of Caesar great *earth* was experienced (d) dearth
18. When Augustus was emperor of Rome *axes* became heavier. (t) taxes
19. Paul instructs Christians to be rooted and *rounded* in love. (g) grounded
20. The voice in the midst of the four beasts said, " a measure of *heat* for a penny." (w) wheat

BUZZING BEES

The leader should prepare copies of sentences for each guest and tell them that they are bees buzzing and they are to make them alight where they should in the following sentences. A tiny jar of honey would be an ideal gift for the winner.

1. The gate of the temple was called Be............. . (Beautiful
2. To a Christian all things are be........... new. (become)
3. A man does not light a candle and put it under a be...... . (bed)
4. In the be............. was the word. (beginning)
5. Christians should speak and act on God's be.......... . (behalf)
6. Christians should be sober and of good be.......... . (behavior)
7. John the Baptist was be.............(beheaded)
8. Our Father has be............. us with love. (bestowed)
9. The centurion came be............... Jesus. (beseeching)

10. Be............... was the birthplace of Jesus. (*Bethlehem*)
11. Christians be.......... to Christ. (*belong*)
12. The serpent be.............. Eve. (*beguiled*)
13. Christians should be............ of false prophets. (*beware*)

Conversation Games

LET DOWN

Players are seated in a circle. The leader tells players that they must do exactly as he does. The leader begins the game by crossing his legs as he says, "My name is Simeon, and I'm going to let down my net to catch fish." When the leader says, "let down," he must uncross his legs. As players take turns the leader will soon know how obvious to make the uncrossing of his legs. The players will soon catch this part of the act, of course, thinking that they have discovered the secret. They will be surprised when the leader has them sit on the floor because the secret is in the position of the arms and hands which must be in a *let down* position (hands may rest on the chair to divert attention, but arms must be *let down* on either side). Any player failing to assume this position must sit on the floor.

TIE — THE (TITHE)

Players sit in a circle. Leader tells players that the game has to do with Tie-thing (Tithing), and that players must do as she says and does or sit on the floor. The leader starts the game by saying, "I have my tie. The (tithe) question is, do you have yours?" She says this because she is wearing shoes with strings that *tie*. The secret being that if a player is wearing any *thing* that *ties:* such as shoes with strings, a tie belt, a bow in the hair or on the dress or a man's tie, he has his *tie*. Of course, in directing the question to the player on his right, he must be careful to pronounce *T-h-e* as though it belonged with the *tie* making it sound as the word *tithe*. The next player may answer, "No, I do not have my *Tie-the* question is, Do you have yours?" He says this because he is not wearing anything that ties. The only rule is that the tie must be visible to other players. A bow on the back of a dress would not count. As the leader starts the game she may wish to make some sort of gestures with the hands to further confuse players.

EMPTY CHAIR

Girls are seated on chairs in a circle. One chair is empty. A boy stands behind each chair including the vacant chair. The boy behind the vacant chair points to a girl and says, "I want you in my chair." He directs a question to the boy standing behind the girl. If the boy cannot answer the question correctly the girl in his chair must get up and go to the vacant chair and the game continues with a boy at the empty chair asking the next question and so on. Questions should be related to the New Testament and Christian teachings. Leader should be familiar with the New Testament and keep one handy to verify answers. Leader may allow boy to whom the question is directed to consult briefly with the girl in his chair as to the answer. Examples of questions: In what city was Jesus born? Who was Elizabeth? What was the name of the angel who visited Marry? Who was Stephen? If the boy to whom the question is directed answers correctly, the boy behind the empty chair must point to another girl and repeat the saying, but must always ask a different question of the boy.

PASSOVER

The leader makes a copy of the following story and begins by telling players that they must read the story exactly as she does. Players who fail will drop out of the game. The secret is in the last line which is actually not a part of the story but when a player gets to the last line he simply says the last line and at the same time passes the paper over to the next player. The word *this* means the paper on which the story is written. It is passed over to the next player.

The Passover was a great festival to celebrate the Exodus from Egypt. It was when the Lord passed over the first-born of the Hebrews and smote those of the Egyptians. A lamb was roasted whole, not a bone of it broken. It was eaten entirely on the same night; if not all eaten, the remainder was burned. The blood of the lamb was sprinkled on the door post.

This is the story. Pass Over.

SENTENCE HOPPING

Players sit in a circle. Leader starts the game by saying a sentence. This may be anything related to a person or thing in the New Testament. Example: "Stephen was the first Christian martyr." The player next to the leader's left must make another sentence regarding Stephen and also use the first letter of his name in another word in the sentence. For instance, he might say, "Stephen stood firm for Christ." The next player must continue in the same manner using the letter S in a different way in another sentence and so on. He might say, "Stephen was stoned." When all the players have had a turn the second player forms a new sentence and game continues in like manner, always using the first letter of the subject. Player who fails to make a sentence must sit on the floor and is given a chance to resume his seat on the next question around. Answers must be given rather quickly.

TALENTS

This game originated from the parable of the ten talents. The leader will need to prepare in advance a small wallet containing ten slips of paper. Players are seated in a circle. The leader explains that the game has to do with a master going away and leaving talents to his servants. He tells players they are to watch him and then do and say exactly as he does. Of course, the number of talents may be more than his. The leader begins the game by taking all the slips of papers from the wallet except one. He places the papers in his lap and, holding the wallet in the air, he says, "My Master went away and left me only one talent." Naturally the players will think the secret is in how many papers are left in the wallet when actually this has nothing to do with it. The secret is in the position of the fingers. Representing the one talent, the leader must have one finger extended while the other fingers are closed. His hand may be in any position as long as it is visible to the players. The leader then places the papers back in the wallet and hands it to the next player. This player might remove all papers except three and say, "My Master went away and left me only three talents." This, of course, would not be correct unless the player also had three fingers extended. Players who fail must stand in the center. They may be given a chance to resume their seat by any player who hands them the wallet. Leader may have a helper who knows the secret. Slips of papers must be large enough so that players can easily count them as they are taken from the wallet.

MY INCIDENT

Guests are seated in a circle. The leader starts the game by telling of an incident given in the New Testament. When he has finished he must conclude by saying, "My incident." The player who can answer first with a person or place related to this incident may continue by relating another incident. For example: If the leader says, "The birth of Jesus is My incident," Incident is the signal for any of the group to answer provided he or she knows a person or place connected with the incident. In this instance, answering players would yell, "Place, Bethlehem," or perhaps he might say, "Person, Marry." Answering player must then relate an incident and the game continues in the same manner. Incidents must be brief and to the point and must always end with, "My incident." Players must always preface answers with category of person or place. Failure to do so will disqualify and the player who is second is allowed to answer.

MY NAME IS PAUL

Players are seated in a circle. The leader says, "My name is Paul and I'm going on a missionary journey." He must say *a* journey because this is his first journey. The player next to him is his helper and must be informed secretly before the game starts. Second player says, "My name is Paul and I'm going on a missionary journey too." The *too* (two) is the catch in the game because this tells that Paul is on the second missionary journey, which in this instance is correct with leader having already taken the first missionary journey (a). The leader explains that unless players say the sentence correctly they must sit on the floor. The correct sentence for the third player would be "My name is Paul and I'm going on *a* missionary journey." If third player says, "I'm going on a missionary journey *too*," he must sit on the floor. *Too* must always follow *a* as Paul must take the first journey before he can take the second. After this is played for several minutes, leader may wish to help players solve the mystery by adding, "My name is Paul and I'm going on a missionary journey to Galatia." Second player (helper) would say, "My name is Paul and I'm going on a missionary journey to Greece." Surely players would soon recognize the names of the places of Paul's first and second missionary journeys.

REPTILE OR INSECT

Each player is given eight or more slips of paper on which are written the names of a kind of reptile or insect. Leader should prepare these in advance. The same names are given to each player but not in any particular order. Players are seated on the floor facing each other. There must be an even number as a player plays in opposition to the one across from him. Players place papers in a row on the floor in front of them with names turned down. When the leader blows the whistle the game begins by the first two players at the head of the line picking up a paper from his row and turning it over, name up for all to see. If the two names that are turned up by the players are alike in the same category, players must immediately call, "Reptile, Insect" and whatever the two names turned up comes under they must say also. Example: If both players turned up the word *snake*, players must yell, "Reptile, insect, reptile." If players succeed in doing this, each is allowed two points. If the names are the same and either player fails to immediately call his category he must forfeit that slip to the other player which will count for the other player in the final score and against the losing player. When a player gains a slip of paper he merely lays it to the side of his others, name down. When a player forfeits a slip of paper, leader must supply him with another on which is written the same name. Leader must keep an account of papers given out to player as these will count a point each against that player. If player turns up a name which is not the same as his opponent but is in the same category he is allowed one point, but only if he calls the correct category. Example: If one player turned up the name *bee*, his opponent turned up *gnat,* the category would be *insect.* The first player to recognize the category and call it is given the point. In case of a tie, both players are given a point. When turning up papers, players must not lift them from the floor other than just to turn them over. When players have had their turn they must always turn slips face down on the floor as in the original position regardless of play. Game continues down the line by each player and his opponent taking turns in like manner. After the first few plays, players will have fun testing their memory by trying to remember where the names are which have been turned up. Leader may set a time period for this game. Other players may assist leader in giving fair score or better still, a scorekeeper should be chosen to help the leader. In addition to the points mentioned, leader also gives an extra five points to each player for every slip of paper he has over the eight given him at the start of the game.

A suitable prize would be an artificial insect which can be purchased at any five-and-ten-cent store.

Examples of names of insects and reptiles are:

(Insects) gnat, grasshopper, hornet, lice, ant, bee, cankerworm, caterpillar, cricket, horseleech and crimson.

(Reptiles) adder, asp, basilisk, cockatrice, chamelion, coral, dragon, lizard, gecko, snail and scorpion.

To make the game more difficult and to learn the names, leader may use some names in the original Hebrew translation.

(Insects) Ch*a*rgol is a beetle; ch*a*ga*b* is a grasshopper; *Gaza*m is a caterpillar; tze*la*tz*a*l is a locust; ash is a moth and *akkabi*sh is a spider.

(Reptile) V*i*per is a serpent; sheph*i*ph*o*n is an adder; s*a*r*a*ph is a serpent; a*gra*b is a scorpion and le*taa*h is a lizard.

BEFORE AND AFTER

Players are seated in a circle. The leader is seated with them. He holds up an empty matchbox. The leader opens the box and explains that when the box is open it represents Paul's life before his conversion. He closes the box and explains that when it is closed it represents Paul's life after his conversion. He tells players that he is going to pass the matchbox around and each player must pass it and say and do exactly as he does. It may be passed open or closed, but it must be done correctly or players must sit on the floor. The leader must have one player or more who knows the secret to sit on his right. The leader may start by holding the matchbox open in his left hand and as he passes it to the player on his right he says, "I pass this to you symbolic of Paul before his conversion." As the leader hands the matchbox with his left hand to the player on his right, the players will naturally think that the secret is either in passing it with the left hand or how far the box is opened. However, the secret is what is being done with the other hand. If the leader passes the matchbox open, the index finger and thumb of his right hand must be pressed together as if he were striking a match. The right hand may be in any position as long as the fingers are pressed together and the hand is visible to the other players. This represents Paul trying to destroy and striking against Christians (taking a match from the open box and getting ready to strike it). The helper may pass the box in the same way or he may close the box and pass it with his right as he says, "I pass this to you symbolic of Paul's new life after his conversion." In this case, the secret is in keeping the left hand open (not being in a position to strike a match). This implies that Paul is no longer striking against Christians and has closed his old life. Players will be confused as the leader watches closely and has them sit on the floor when they fail to pass the matchbox correctly. When a player fails, the box is returned to the leader and it is passed again. A player may have a chance to get off the floor when he is sure that he can pass the box in the correct way.

HONESTY PAYS

Honesty or pay the penalty — Players are seated in a circle. Everyone must tell the truth or pay the penalty. Penalties may be anything designed by the leader. The leader begins the game by asking any one of the group a simple Bible question. Example: "Do you know how many books there are in the New Testament?" If the player knows the number of books he would simply answer, "Yes." Players must be careful of their answers because any player in the group may challenge the one being asked to give proof of the answer. If player answers honestly he gets to ask the person beside him the next question. If player refuses to or cannot answer the question he must pay the penalty and the leader must ask someone another question. All questions must be related to the New Testament in some manner.

SECRET TITLE

Players sit in a circle. The leader starts the game by saying, "I know another title for Christ beginning with the letter C. Do you?" He points his finger to a player in the group who must answer quickly with a title beginning with C. When the player gives his title, the leader must then respond by revealing his secret title. The player answering becomes the leader and repeats the statement. He may choose to use the same statement with a different name and letter. For example, he might say, "I know another title for our Saviour beginning with the letter S. Do you?" In any event, the letter chosen must always be the same as the first letter of the title in the statement. In this instance, the secret title might be "Seed of David" or "Shepherd." If the answering player and the leader should have the same title, the leader must make another statement choosing a different secret title. If a player fails to answer when pointed to, he must sit on the floor and the leader points to someone else. Leader may give players on the floor a chance to resume their seats after all the players have had a turn. A prize may be given to the player who knows the most titles. Numerous titles may be found in the cyclopedia index of the Bible.

Listed are some titles:

Bread of Life	Bishop of Souls
Bridegroom	Bread of Heaven
Beloved	Chief Shepherd
Begotten of the Father	Chosen of God
Beloved of God	Christ
Babe	Christ, the King

Christ Jesus

Christ the Lord

Corner-Stone

First Born

Friend of Sinners

Forerunner

Firstfruits

Finisher of Faith

Faithful Witness

Firstborn of every Creature

First and Last

Jesus

Jesus Christ

Jesus Christ our Lord

Jesus Christ our Saviour

Jesus of Nazareth

Jesus, Son of God

Jesus, Son of Joseph

Just Man

Just One

Just Person

Lamb

Life

Light

Light of the World

Living Bread

Living Stone

Lord

Lord Christ

Lord Jesus

Lord from Heaven

Lord of All

Lord of Glory

Salvation

Samaritan

Sanctification

Savior of the Body

Son of David

Son of God

Savior of the World

Second Man

Seed of David

Shepherd

Shepherd of Souls

Read Games

WHO WAS PAUL?

Leader may read the following, omitting the italicized words. Object is for players to fill in the blanks.

Paul was born at *Tarsus,* capital of *Cilicia.* He was a *tentmaker.* He was taught by Gamaliel. Paul persecuted the *Christians.* He went to *Damascus* to arrest them. On the way, a bright *light* from *heaven* blinded him. *Jesus* appeared to him. He was led into the city where he remained *blind* for *three* days. God restored his sight through *Ananias.* Paul was *baptized* and became an *apostle* for *Christ, preaching* and *teaching* until his death.

NAME THE BOOK

Name the Book is played by the leader calling out sentences and players giving the correct book in the New Testament to which each sentence refers or is found. A score-keeper may keep score, giving a player one point for each correct answer. Player must stand when he or she knows the answer. Answers are in parenthesis.

1. A message to seven churches. (Revelation)
2. Believers, living stones built into a temple. (I Peter)
3. Imprisoned apostle thankful for friends at Philippi. (Philippians)
4. Sermon on the Mount. (Matthew)
5. Feeding the five thousand. (Mark)
6. Position of women in the church. (I Corinthians)
7. Stephen's arrest. (Acts)
8. Raising of Lazarus. (John)
9. Paul's three missionary journeys. (Acts)
10. Murder of John the Baptist. (Mark)
11. Warnings against false teachers. (I Timothy)
12. Seventh seal and the seven trumpets. (Revelation)
13. Birth of John the Baptist. (Luke)
14. The Last Supper. (Matthew)

15. Instructions Titus gives to classes. (Titus)
16. Shipwreck of Paul. (Acts)
17. Peter's release from prison. (Acts)
18. Salvation is a free gift. (Romans)

IT IS SO — YES OR NO

Leader may read statements to players and have them raise their hands to answer or ask them to stand when answering. If player answers correctly he may remain standing and try to answer the next statement. When player fails to answer correctly he must sit down. Answers are in parenthesis.

1. The word *leisure* is only used once in the Bible. (yes) Mark 6:31
2. Easter is not mentioned in the Bible. (no) Once in Acts 12:4
3. Herod was eaten of worms. (yes) Acts 12:23
4. Judas Iscariot was eaten by worms too. (no) Matthew 27:5
5. Gamaliel was a physician. (no) Acts 5:34
6. Satan is compared to a roaring lion. (yes) I Peter 5:8
7. John was known as Simon. (no)
8. Peter was sometimes called Cephas. (yes) John 1:42
9. Handkerchiefs were used by Paul to heal the sick. (yes) Acts 19:11, 12
10. The word school is mentioned several times in the Bible. (no) Only once Acts 19:9
11. The book of Mark states that Jesus sang a song with His disciples. (yes) A hymn, Mark 14:26
12. Zenas was a lawyer. (yes) Titus 3:13
13. A townclerk brought order in an assembly of confusion in Ephesus where Paul's companions had been taken. (yes) Acts 19:35
14. Once during Paul's preaching Eutychus went to sleep and fell from a window. (yes) Acts 20:9

WHAT-A-YA-KNOW

What-a-Ya-Know is a quiz game. Give each guest a sheet of paper and a pencil and read each question, allowing time to write the answers. Questions may be typed, a copy for each guest, if the leader prefers. When questions have been answered, leaders may read correct answers and let guests check their own paper. Ten minutes is enough time to allow. Give prize to the player with the most correct answers. A pocket dictionary would be a suitable prize.

1. Who was Luke?
    (The writer of a gospel and of the Acts. He was a physician. Born at Antioch)
2. Who was Caesar Augustus?
    (First emperor of Rome)
3. What is repentance?
    (Sorrow for sin. A change of mind and heart)
4. Who was Elias?
    (Elijah the Prophet)
5. What language is the word "Rabbi"?
    (Hebrew)
6. To whom was the Sermon on the Mount addressed?
    (To the disciples of Jesus)
7. What is meant by the harvest?
    (The judgment)
8. Who are the Reapers?
    (The angels)
9. What will happen to the tares?
    (They will be burned)
10. Who are the tares?
    (The children of the wicked one)
11. To whom did our Lord appear first after His resurrection?
    (To Mary Magdalene and Mary the mother of James)
12. At what time was the "third hour of the day"?
    (At nine A.M.)
13. What time was the ninth hour?
    (Three P.M.)
14. Who is the prince of this world?
    (Satan, who rules over the evil spirits of the earth and in the hearts of men)
15. What does it mean to "hallow" something?
    (To treat it holy)

16. By whom are we born again?
    (By the Holy Spirit)
17. What was our Lord's solemn object in coming into this world?
    (To lay down His life in order to give us life)
18. Should Christians expect not to have trouble?
    (No, it is only "through much tribulation" that we can "enter into the kingdom of God.")

WORDS WITH A DIFFERENT MEANING

Leader may wish to give hints if players have difficulty grasping game.

1. What word in a parable is used on a hot dog?   (mustard)
2. What word in a parable is a dog?   (shepherd)
3. What word in a parable is a ship?   (vessel)
4. What word in a parable is worn on the wrist   (watch)
5. What word in a parable is a measuring device?   (ruler)
6. What word in a parable is what we breathe?   (heir)
7. What word in a parable is part of a knife?   (blade)
8. What word in a parable is a small stream?   (branch)
9. What word in a parable is where tourists stay?   (lodge)
10. What word in a parable is a fabric used in wedding gowns?
                                                        (net)

SNEAKY WORDS

Give each player a New Testament and as the leader reads the following sentences, players are to find the answers in the Scripture verses given. A tiny Bible would be a suitable prize.

1. The name of a well-known brush company is found in Mark 9:3. (Fuller)
2. The name of a boy is found in Romans 8:19. (Ernest)
3. Something the weather is on a clear day, Acts 7:20. (fair)
4. A part of our body, Mark 4:28. (ear)
5. The last part of a story, Matthew 24:3. (end)
6. Something one does to stay healthy, Acts 24:16. (exercise)
7. Something we do to dismiss a person from a position, Matthew 25:41. (fire)

8. A part of a diver's suit, Ephesians 6:17. (helmet)
9. Something most everyone does at a football game, I Thessalonians 4:16. (shout)
10. Something a woman does to her hose, Matthew 13:25. (tares)
11. Something a baby soon gets, Matthew 5:38. (tooth)
12. Something we call a confused noice, Matthew 26:5. (uproar)
13. Something we like to have in our hair, Matthew 14:24. (waves)
14. Something we do to our floors, Hebrews 1:11. (wax)
15. The name of an animal, Matthew 3:11. (bear)
16. Something most women are interested in, (I Corinthians 7:31. (fashion)
17. A method of transporting goods, Hebrews 1:3. (express)

LIFE WITH GRACE

Give each guest a pencil and paper and as the leader reads, players may answer in own words or quote Scripture verses in answering. Leader may allow players to use their Bibles; however, a time limit should be set with or without the use of the Bible. Sentences may be copied for players if leader so desires.

1. When does Grace help us in talking?
   ("Let your speech be always with grace" (Colossians 4:6.)
2. When does Grace tell what we are?
   ("By the grace of God I am what I am" (I Corinthians 15:10.)
3. When does Grace bring peace?
   ("Grace to you and peace from God" (Romans 1:7.)
4. When can we find Grace waiting with something at the throne?
   ("Let us come boldly unto the throne of grace, that we may obtain mercy, and find grace to help in time of need" (Hebrews 4:16.)
5. How can Grace determine our height.
   ("Grow in grace" II Peter 3:18.)

6. How can Grace assist us in song?
   ("Singing with grace" (Colossians 3:16.)
7. Who is in authority over all the graces?
   ("The God of all grace" I Peter 5:10.)
8. How is Grace glorified?
   ("The glory of his grace" Ephesians 1:6.)
9. How can Grace save us?
   ("We believe that through the grace of the Lord Jesus Christ we shall be saved" Acts 15:11.)
10. When is Grace wealthy?
    ("The riches of his grace" Ephesians 1:7.)
11. Is Grace all we need?
    ("My grace is sufficient for thee" II Corinthians 12:9.)
12. When is Grace invisible?
    ("The Spirit of grace" Hebrews 10:29.)
13. When does Grace act as an officer?
    ("Justified by his grace" Titus 3:7.)
14. When does Grace introduce us to Faith?
    ("By grace ye are saved through faith" Ephesians 2:8.)
15. When does Grace deliver a message?
    ("The word of his grace" Acts 20:32.)
16. When will we meet a new grace?
    ("Hope to the end for the grace that is to be brought to you at the Revelation of Christ" I Peter 1:13.)

Name Games

NAME THE CHARACTER

Can you give the name of the person in the New Testament who spoke these words?

1. "Can there any good thing come out of Nazareth?"
   (Nathanael)
2. "Behold the Lamb of God." (John the Baptist)
3. "Lord, dost thou wash my feet?" (Simon Peter)
4. "Lord, dost thou not care that my sister hath left me to serve alone? bid her therefore that she help me." (Martha)
5. "Understandest thou what thou readest?" (Philip)
6. "Behold the handmaid of the Lord, be it unto me according to thy word." (Mary, mother of Jesus)
7. "The Lord hath raised up an horn of salvation for us in the house of his servant, David." (Zacharias)
8. "What accusation bring ye against this man?" (Pilate)
9. "How can a man be born when he is old?" (Nicodemus)
10. "Art thou he that should come, or do we look for another?"
    (John the Baptist)

BOY'S NAME PLUS

1. A boy's name plus one letter is where the corpse of John the Baptist was placed. (*tomb*)
2. A name plus seven letters was burned as incense.
   (*frank*incense)
3. A name plus three letters is what the daughter of Herodias did to please the king . (*danced*)
4. A skill often used by man to form idols of gold is also a boy's three letter name. (art)
5. A name plus four letters is what charity does. (*edifys*)
6. A name plus three letters tells why the olive tree is wild. (*nature*)
7. Two names tell how some people observe the same things. (Alike, Al & Ike)

48

8. A name plus one letter is what every Christian should learn to use wisely. (*time*)
9. A name plus one letter tells what God is always. (*same*)
10. A name plus five letters are things Christians should not be too concerned about. (*material*)

HIDDEN BOOKS

The names of certain books in the New Testament are hidden in the following sentences. Leader should supply each guest with a pencil and a copy of the sentences listed, omitting the emphaisis on the letters which reveal the answers. A clue is that after finding the first letter of the name, the other letters follow in succession.

1. I'm going to *Mar*y's *k*itchen shower tomorrow. (Mark)
2. Did you know that *L*ibby can play the *uke*? (Luke)
3. *He brews* delicious coffee.(Hebrews)
4. Please place the *mat* on *the w*alk. (Matthew)
5. The *ties* are *moth* eaten and *y*ellow. (Timothy)
6. *Phil* cut his *lip* and *I am near* shock. (Philippians)
7. There are many reasons why *Velvet* can't run *in* the race *on* Tuesday. (Revelation)
8. A *cat* ran *s*traight across the road in front of my car. (Acts)
9. *R*uth *o*rders *most* of her *anklets* from Chicago. (Romans)
10. *Jan* and *Mes*redith are such dear friends. (James)
11. *J*ack *ow*es *h*im *n*ineteen dollars. (John)
12. *J*erry *used* to deliver the paper. (Jude)
13. *Tim took us* to dinner last night. (Titus)
14. The *col*urt *deals* with the serious crimes *in any* state. (Colossians)
15. Will you *please* empty *every* wastebasket? (Peter)
16. If you can *g*ive me *all* the d*ates I can* study them. (Galatians)
17. *Cora intends* to *help Ivan* study. (Corinthians)
18. The *phone is in Ann's* room. (Ephesians)
19. *The* table s*tool* straight after *Lonnie and* Steve fixed it. (Thessalonians)
20. The *police hit Clem on* the head. (Philemon)

"X" CITIES

Give each guest a sheet of paper and a pencil and have them list as many cities as they can that are mentioned in the New Testament. Guests naming the most of those marked with an X should receive a special prize.

Cities mentioned are:

Antioch	Chorazin X	Nazareth
Alexandria	Corinth	Nineveh X
Athens	Dalmanutha X	Rome
Berea	Ephesus	Sidon X
Bethlehem	Iconium X	Tarshish X
Bethany	Jerusalem	Tarsus
Bethsaida X	Joppa	Troas
Capernaum	Lystra X	Thessalonica X
Caesarea	Miletus X	

TITLE CONTEST

Give guests paper and a pencil and ask them to write as many titles applied to Jesus Christ and mentioned in the New Testamen as they can think of. The leader will need to have handy a Bible with cyclopedia index to check answers, as there are over 175 listed. Better still, the leader might look them up in advance and make a copy. Guests getting names that are not so familiar should be given an extra prize and of course, the guest getting the most titles should be given a prize.

Some unusual titles are:

Advocate	Holy Thing
Apostle of Our Profession	Horn of Salvation
Bishop of Souls	Judge of Quick and Dead
Brazen Serpent	Just Man
Consolation of Israel	Just One
Creditor	Melchizedec
Dayspring from on High	Potentate
Daystar	Propitiation.
Golden Altar	Quickening Spirit
Governor	Surety
Holy, Harmless, and Undefiled	Testator

MEASURE OF LOVE

Give guests paper and pencil. Have them write as many descriptive words as they can think of that are mentioned in the New Testament in reference to God and His love for us. Do not allow more than ten minutes.

Here is a list:

Spirit	Gracious	Longsuffering
Compassionate	Great	Loving
Faithful	Just	Merciful
Holy	Jealous	Glory
Omnipresent	Fruitful	Kind
Perfect	Eternal	Unfailing
Tender	Living Grace	Goodness
Righteous	Restful	Slow to anger
True	Peace	Power
Life	Great	

Give a prize of a tape measure to the guest having the longest list.

NAME THE THING

Give out slips of paper on which the following names are written. Players are to write the thing the name represents. The answers are things used or mentioned in the New Testament. Leader may wish to give the answer to one as an example. Give a prize to the one having the largest number correct in the time period set by the leader.

1.	Morton	1.	(salt)
2.	Flash	2.	(light)
3.	Irish	3.	(linen)
4.	Cannon	4.	(towel)
5.	Bordens	5.	(milk)
6.	King	6.	(fish)
7.	Bath	7.	(robe)
8.	Red Goose	8.	(shoes)
9.	Whole wheat	9.	(bread)
10.	Playtex	10.	(girdle)

11.	Fish	11.	(hook)
12.	Police	12.	(officer)
13.	Swimming	13.	(pool)
14.	Front	14.	(porch)
15.	Flower	15.	(pot)
16.	Pogo	16.	(stick)
17.	Writing	17.	(tablet)
18.	School	18.	(teacher)
19.	New	19.	(Testament)
20.	Grocery	20.	(store)

WHO SAID?

Leader should prepare in advance copies of the following for each guest.

1. "If thou wilt, let us make here three tabernacles; one for thee, and one for Moses, and one for Elias." (Peter)
2. "Lord, they know that I imprisoned and beat in every synagogue them that believed on thee." (Paul)
3. "Behold, I see the heavens opened, and the Son of Man standing on the right hand of God." (Stephen)
4. "Understandest thou what thou readest?" (Philip)
5. "If ye have judged me to be faithful to the Lord, come into my house and abide there." (Lydia)
6. "Four days ago I was fasting until this hour; and at the ninth hour I prayed in my house, and, behold, a man stood before me in bright clothing." (Cornelius)
7. "Verily, verily, I say unto you, I am the door of the sheep." (Jesus)
8. "I am the voice of one crying in the wilderness." (John the Baptist)
9. "Behold, this child is set for the fall and rising again of many in Israel." (Simeon)
10. "Son, why hast thou thus dealt with us? behold, thy father and I have sought thee sorrowing." (Mary, mother of Jesus)

FLOWERS IN MASQUERADE

Names of flowers are hidden in the following sentences. A clue is that after finding the first letter of the name in a sentence, the other letters of that name follow in succession. Example: In the third sentence we find *carna* in the first word and the remainder of the flower name is found in the second word, gratification, thus making the name *carnation*. Leader should prepare written copies of sentences in advance. An appropriate prize for the winner would be an artificial flower or a real flower. If the winner is a boy he is given the flower and must present it to his favorite girl. This should be a secret until the winner is announced. Leader may request boy to make a speech when making the presentation, such as: "You are the flower of my life," and etc.

Sentences are as follows:

1. Jesus a*rose* from the tomb. (rose)
2. Gethsemane was the name of a *garden in a*n area near Mt. Olivet. (gardenia)
3. *Carnal* gratification is fleshly frailty. (carnation)
4. The hon*or which* we *give* is more than wor*d.* (orchid)
5. The *tru*th never s*lips.* (tulip)
6. A *morning* prayer *glori*fies our da*y.* (morning glory)
7. Many people to*day* live in hypocris*y.* (daisy)
8. Paul *went* faith*fully* to Macedo*nia.* (petunia)
9. He will *pardon* us today. (pansy)
10. We *must* be humble. (mum)
11. Jesus said, "Do *viole*nce *to* no man." (violet)
12. Let us *live* our *li*fe the right wa*y.* (lily)
13. *Iscariot* betrayed Christ. (iris)
14. They were *astonished* at His doctrine. (aster)
15. *Pontius* Pilate and the *people* betrayed Him. (poppy)

NAME A BODY

Give players blank sheets of paper and a pencil and tell them to write the names of as many different kinds of religious denominations as they can think of. Since there are more than 254 different bodies, the leader should set a time limit for this game. Be sure to give an extra prize to the player naming the most unheard-of denominations. Example: The Church of Illumination is not as familiar to us as the many Baptist bodies.

Some of the churches are:

Congregational	Pentecostal	Mennonite
Disciples of Christ	Open Bible	Lutheran
Eastern Orthodox	Quaker	Latter-day Saints
Christadelphians	Salvation Army	Jewish
Brethren	The Schwenkfelder	Holiness
Buddhist	Social Brethren	Greek Orthodox
Catholic	Spiritualists	Church of Christ
Methodist	Mormon	Christian
Evangelistic	Moslems	Pilgrim Holiness
Church of Illumination	Moravian	Vedanta Society
Jehovah's Witnesses	Friends	Universalists

Active Games

SCRATCH OUT LOVE

One player is selected to be Scratch. If there is a large group there should be two Scratches. Players join hands and form a circle. Scratch is in the center. The leader acts as the reader and as he reads continually I Corinthians, chapter 13, players walk slowly around Scratch who is standing still. When the reader says the word *charity*, players must stop, drop hands and stoop. Scratch tries to tag a player in the circle before he can get in a stooped position. If he succeeds the player tagged changes places with him and becomes Scratch and the game continues. If Scratch fails to tag a player, players resume their original position and reader continues to read. Reader may use the word *love* in several places instead of *charity* as he reads and only say, "Charity," when he wishes players to stop.

PENNY FOR A THOUGHT

Players sit in a circle. The leader has two or more cards for each player prepared in advance. Approximate size cards should be six by six inches. The leader writes any feat he chooses on each card, but they must be related in some way to Scriptures. For example: On one card may be, "Name the apostles." There should be an assortment of things to do such as Quote John 3:16 or act out a certain Scripture verse and etc. These cards are arranged face down on the floor around a bowl. Cards on which are written simple feats should be colored red on the top side. Others are not colored. The leader gives the starting player a penny and when he blows the whistle, the player tries to pitch penny into bowl. If the player misses he must pick up the card upon which the penny has dropped and must carry out the request written on it. The player hands penny to the person on his left and the game continues in the same manner. After each feat is performed card is kept by the player or collected by the leader. Of course, the player who throws the penny into the bowl the most times is the winner. An appropriate prize would be a small bank and also the penny used in the game. Ten minutes is long enough to play unless the group is quite large. A large bowl is used, as players must remain seated while pitching the penny.

CATCH THE PLATE

Players are seated in a circle. The leader gives each player a name of a person from the New Testament. Each player must remember his name. Then the leader stands in the center of the group and twirls the plate. As he spins he calls a name. The one who has this name must catch the plate before it comes to a stop. If he fails to do so he must pay a penalty.

FAMILY

Leader reads the following names to guests and tells them that each may choose any name called but not to reveal the name chosen. Babes, good fishes, good servants, light, stones, salt, sun, wheat, branches, members, brothers, disciples, children, runners, soldiers, pearls, wrestlers or vessels. Players sit in chairs in a circle. The leader stands in the center and says: "God's people are referred to in the Bible in many ways. They are called, sheep, salt, sun, wheat and vessels and etc. But I would rather be called a Christian. I am in a family." When the leader calls a name which is represented by a player, that player must get up, turn his chair around and sit down with his back toward the group. Every time his name is called he must rise and turn his chair. When the leader says, "Christian," all players must place their chairs in the original position and when he says, "Family," all players change seats. The leader must try to get a chair when the change is taking place as this is really the main object of the game. The player left standing when the others are seated becomes the leader and he tells about God's people in the same way. The leader may say the sentences as slowly or as rapidly as he wishes.

MY HAT, JOHN

Players are seated in a circle. One player named John stands in the center. The leader whispers a name to each player. The name must be one of the four Gospels, either Matthew, Mark, Luke or John. Do not give the names in the proper order to players in the circle. For example, the person next to Matthew could be named Luke or another Matthew. Players must remember their names. Each player wears a paper hat except the player in the center. When the leader blows the whistle, the player in the center must try to get out of center into the circle by finding the four gospel names in their proper order. Example: Player points to someone and says, "My Hat, Matthew," but if the person happens to be Mark or any other name, he would answer, "My Hat, Mark," or whatever his name is. John cannot start correctly until he points to someone named Matthew, since this is the first book of the four gospels. Then he must find the remainder in succession — Matthew, Mark, Luke and John. The player will find it difficult to remember the names of players which he has uncovered in his search for Matthew. When the player in the center has succeeded in completing the gospels and has found them in their proper order with the last one pointed to being "My Hat, John," this John must exchange places with the John in the circle and the game continues. After playing in this manner several minutes players names may be changed by the leader. A prize may be given to the player who is quickest to get out of the circle by completing the four gospels. A derby hat would be a suitable prize. At the close of the game players are allowed to keep their paper hats and of course, leader will want to have an extra hat for player in the center who starts the game.

POST OFFICE

You will need a rather large box. Print in large letters the name post office on the side and place the box at the far end of the room. You will also need several small envelopes and slips of paper, allowing about four for each player. Write a verse of Scripture that has been selected from one of the epistles (Romans, Hebrews or any other) on each piece of paper. Leader should give one of these papers and several envelopes to each player before starting the game. Papers should be large enough to fold over and slide into the envelope as you would a letter. When the leader gives the signal, players must address the envelopes to whom the epistle verse is written. Example: "For all have sinned and come short of the glory of God" would go in an envelope addressed to the Romans. Be sure that each player has a pencil and have them sign their name in the upper left corner of the envelope. Each envelope must be sealed before player takes it to the post office. After mailing the first letter, player rushes back to leader for another Scripture verse which he takes care of in the same manner. When the final letter is mailed the leader checks the box and counts the letters each person has mailed. Letters not having a return address (name of player) will go into the dead letter box and will not be counted. Of course, Scripture verse must also be in the correct book or letter will be disqualified. In this instance, the address on each envelope represents that book. Leader may appoint two players to assist him as mail clerks. A prize may be given to the one mailing the most letters. A letter opener or a box of stationary would be a suitable prize. A consolation prize of a five cent stamp may be given the one with the least number of letters mailed.

PIN THE SCRIPTURE IN THE BOOK

Print the names (rather large) of the books of the four gospels on a piece of cardboard approximately 12 x 20, leaving about four inches space between each name. Select several Scripture verses (about five for each player) from the four gospels and print or type each on a small slip of paper. Tack the cardboard on the wall and give each player five of these Scripture verses. Taking turns, let players pin one strip at a time in the correct gospel or book. Players must remember to write their names on the verses as the leader will want to check and see how many verses were pinned in the correct book. Several small prizes may be needed as there may be more than one winner. Book markers make nice, inexpensive prizes.

PUZZLE PICTURE

Get several Bible pictures — one for each guest. Cut each picture into ten or twelve pieces and put the pieces in an envelope. When all is ready, give each player an envelope and when the leader gives the signal players are to assemble the picture. Players should sit on the floor and place the picture in front of them. Leader may give a prize to the winner or purchase inexpensive picture puzzles from a Bible bookstore, letting guests exchange pictures and keep them.

A STRING OF BOOKS

Leader should prepare ahead of time slips of paper (strips of typing paper) cut very narrow. There must be twenty-seven strips for each guest. On each paper is written the name of one of the books of the New Testament. Put the twenty-seven slips in an envelope in jumbled manner. Seal the envelopes. Give each guest an envelope and a needle and thread. Needle may or may not be threaded. Guest may not break the seal on his envelope until the leader gives the signal to start the game. The leader explains that each guest is to open his envelope and string the books in their proper order. The leader may call time when he wishes guests to be finished. The guest who gets the most books on his string in the proper order is the winner. A book may be given as a prize to the winner and a package of needles or a spool of thread to the one with lowest number on string.

A MISSING PART

Print Scripture verses on individual cards. Make one or more cards for each guest. Cut cards in half. Keep first half of cards and pin other parts in various places around the room. When guests have arrived, leader gives out parts of cards to guests and tells them to find the missing parts which are somewhere in the room.

GIFTS FOR THE PRODIGAL SON

The leader will need to make preparations in advance by cutting several pictures of things from magazines or old catalogues. These things are to represent gifts which the father might have presented the prodigal son upon his return. There may be several pictures of one item, such as shoes or rings. Before guests arrive the leader should tape the pictures in various areas. Players are asked to make a search for picture gifts. The player finding the largest number is given a prize. A pair of shoe strings or a shoe horn would be an appropriate prize. Pictures of the following may be used: Robes, rings, shoes, cows, meat, bread, milk, butter, or related articles. Players are allowed only a designated time in which to find the pictures.

CONTEST GAMES

CHRISTIAN LEAGUE BOWLING

Write a single question on a half sheet of paper and roll up tightly in pencil fashion. Make five of these rolls for each player. These are the pins. Punch five holes in a piece of cardboard about the size of a dinner plate (or use paper plates) and insert ends of rolled up papers just enough to hold them. Fashion one plate with five pins for each player. Divide players into two equal groups. Each group must choose a captain. Groups are named "The Apostle League" and "The Disciple League." Groups should sit in single lines facing each other. Give each player a cardboard of pins (questions) and tell them they are not to take any of the pins out until it is their turn to bowl. Decide which group is to play first and when the leader blows the whistle the captain of that group selects a question from his board (only one paper at a time). He must unfold and read the question and answer it quickly. Players are allowed only seven seconds in which to answer. If answer is correct he has scored a point for his group. And he may choose another question answering it in the same way. Player may continue to select and answer his questions as long as the leader is satisfied with his answers. Each question answered counts one point and if the player answers all five of the questions on his board in one turn he has scored a total of five points and five points extra for a strike. If player takes a question from his board he cannot answer he must wait for his next turn before selecting another question. It will be better if players sit on the floor and leave their pins in front of them as they select questions. When player has completed his play the player across from him is next and so on until all players have had turns. If any player is able to make a strike and answer all his questions he becomes eligible for new pins which must be ready to refill his plate by the leader. Leader may penalize five points if he finds any one coaching or stealing a look at a question before his turn. Questions should be equally divided as to the simple and difficult. If leader does not wish to prolong the game by giving out more questions when a player has made a strike he may let the player merely assist those on his group in answering their questions instead. However, he may only help during a player's turn. When everyone has played within the time allowed, the leader announces the group with highest score and the winner.

Questions listed are some leader may wish to use. Answers are in parenthesis.

Questions for the Apostles:

1. Name the first book in the New Testament. (Matthew)
2. Where was Jesus born? (Bethlehem)
3. Who wrote the book of Romans? (Paul)
4. Who came before Jesus preaching in the wilderness? (John the Baptist)
5. Who was John's mother? (Elizabeth)
6. Who were the ones bringing gifts to the baby Jesus? (Wise men)
7. In which book is the Sermon on the Mount? (Matthew)
8. Name the sixth book of the New Testament. (Romans)
9. Name books in New Testament beginning with the letter P. (Philippians, Philemon, I Peter, II Peter)
10. How many books are in the New Testament? (twenty-seven)
11. Name the tenth book in the New Testament. (Ephesians)
12. Give the first name of the disciple who betrayed Jesus. (Judas)
13. Name two disciples other than Judas. (Peter and Andrew)
14. Who was the angel who told the Virgin Mary of the coming of the birth of Jesus? (Gabriel)
15. Who wrote the book of Acts? (Luke)
16. Who wrote the book of Luke? (Luke)
17. What was the name of the town where Jesus performed His first miracle? (Cana in Galilee)
18. What was the name of the town in which Jesus lived as a young man? (Nazareth)
19. Who baptized Jesus? (John the Baptist)

20. Where did Joseph and Mary take Jesus at the age of twelve? (Jerusalem)
21. What was the name of the road where Paul was converted? (Damascus)
22. How many apostles were there? (twelve)
23. What was the name of the apostle who doubted? (Thomas)
24. By what methods did Jesus teach? (parables)
25. Name the sister of Mary. (Martha)
26. What was the celebration of the Jewish feast called? (Passover)
27. How many gospels are there? (four)
28. Name the eleventh book of the New Testament. (Philippians)
29. To whom was the Lord's Prayer first given? (the disciples)
30. How many books of Timothy are in the New Testament? (two)
31. Name the only book in the New Testament which starts with the letter G. (Galatians)
32. By what name were the tax collectors known? (publicans)
33. What was Peter's first name? (Simon)
34. What was the name of the well in Samaria where Jesus rested? (Jacob's well)
35. Name the woman who anointed the feet of Jesus with an expensive ointment. (Mary)
36. Where did Jesus say we should lay up treasures? (in heaven)
37. What kind of crown was placed on Jesus before His crucifixion? (crown of thorns)
38. What did they offer Jesus to drink? (vinegar)
39. What is the name given a follower of Christ? (disciple)
40. What kind of bird symbolized the Holy Spirit? (dove)
41. What is called the bride of Christ? (the Church)
42. Give one of the beatitudes? ("Blessed are they that mourn: for they shall be comforted," etc.)

Questions for the Disciples:
1. Name the second book in the New Testament. (Mark)
2. Where did Jesus live as a boy? (Nazareth)

3. Who gave us the Lord's Prayer? (Jesus)
4. What was the name of the mother of Jesus? (Mary)
5. Name the father of John. (Zacharius)
6. To whom was the Sermon on the Mount addressed? (the disciples)
7. Name the third book of the New Testament. (Luke)
8. Name the twelfth book of the New Testament. (Colossians)
9. Name the book next to the last in the New Testament. (Jude)
10. Name books in New Testament which begin with the letter C. (I Corinthians, II Corinthians and Colossians)
11. How many books named John in the New Testament? (four)
12. Name the ninth book in the New Testament. (Galatians)
13. Give the last name of the disciple who betrayed Jesus? (Iscariot)
14. Give another name for Paul. (Saul)
15. Name the angel who told Elizabeth of the coming of John? (Gabriel)
16. Name the last book in the New Testament. (Revelation)
17. What was the name of the king who killed the children in Bethlehem? (Herod)
18. Who was the rich young man Jesus interviewed? (Nicodemus)
19. What was the name of the river in which Jesus was baptized? (Jordan)
20. Where did Joseph and Mary take Jesus to escape the wicked Herod? (Egypt)
21. How many missionary journeys did Paul make? (three)
22. To what tiny seed does Jesus compare the kingdom of heaven? (mustard)
23. What was the name of the brother of Mary who Jesus raised from the dead? (Lazarus)
24. What was the name of the sea where Jesus often taught? (Galilee)
25. Who wrote the book of Galatians? (Paul)

26. Name the eighth book of the New Testament? (II Corinthians)
27. What is the name of the prayer which begins, "Our Father which art in heaven"? (The Lord's Prayer)
28. Name one of Paul's missionary helpers. (Silas)
29. How many books of Corinthians are in the New Testament? (two)
30. What did Jesus say we should do to our enemies? (love them)
31. How many times did Jesus tell Peter that we should forgive our brother? (seventy times seven)
32. How did John the Baptist die? (beheaded)
33. Who is called "The Comforter"? (the Holy Spirit)
34. What color was the robe the soldiers put on Jesus? (purple)
35. What was the place called where the body of Jesus was placed? (sepulchre)
36. What name was given the ordained helpers of Christ? (apostles)
37. What is the word used when one is sorry for sin? (repentance)
38. What is meant by the Trinity? (Father, Son and Holy Spirit)
39. What kind of teaching was "the mote and the beam"? (parable)
40. Who was known as the Good Shepherd? (Christ)
41. Who drove the moneychangers from the Temple? (Jesus)
42. With what letter does the sixth book of the New Testament begin? (R)

THE APOSTLES

Guests are divided into two equal groups. Have each group sit in a line facing each other some distance apart. Each group is named The Apostles. The leader stands in the middle. Leader begins the game by talking aloud about the Apostles. He must call them by name. He may call Judas, Thomas or any of them but when he says, "The apostles," all players must rise from their chairs and rush to the opposite side and find a chair. The object is for the leader to get a chair when the exchange is taking place. The player who does not have a chair when all are seated must take his place in the center. This player becomes the leader and he must start talking in the same way to find a chair. Player in the center may say, "The apostles," whenever he wishes.

SUPER MARKET

Divide players into two equal groups. They are named The Business Group and The Housekeeper Group. Have each group sit in a line facing a goal where the market is located. The market is several feet from the head of the line. The market is arranged by placing fifteen tiny baskets or small boxes around the room either on chairs or on the floor in a manner similar to shelves of canned goods in a super market. Label each box — meat, milk, bread, clothing, coal, corn, cup, dress, drink, feed, garment, vessel, wax, pot, and flower. Leader should have these prepared in advance. Also several Bible references (New Testament only) relating to verses containing each of the above words. These may be found in the concordance of the Bible under the words mentioned. It will require a little preparation but it will be worth the effort. Example: Meat is mentioned in Matthew 6:25, Mark 8:8, Luke 8:55, etc. Write book name, chapter number and verse number on small strips of paper. At least five for each thing listed in the market. Be sure and put the name of the thing the verse represents at the top of each reference. Leader will also need to make fifteen cardboard signs (12 x 12) on which the name of the department is written. Example: *Meat Dept.*, *Clothing Dept.*, etc. These must be hung above or placed against the baskets they represent. Put the reference strips of paper in the proper baskets. You may wish to add other signs such as a large super market sign, sale signs, etc. to add to the fun. Arrange a chair and two tables near the foot, between the lines to represent the check out counter. Leader acts as cashier and sits at this table on which is placed a paper with the names of each group to mark scoring. He will also need three or four New Testaments and a tiny bell and pencils. Leader may choose a player to act as bag boy to assist him in his duties. The leader (cashier) rings the bell and the game begins with the first players in each line going inside the super market and each selecting one slip of paper from any box. The cashier may decide on the time allowed for this selection. He may give them only five seconds. When the cashier calls, "Check out," both players must bring their slips to him. Cashier marks name of merchandise selected on score paper. Example: if player from Business Group selected a strip of paper in the box labeled meat, and player from Housekeepers Group selected bread, the cashier would simply put meat under Business Group and bread under Housekeepers Group. While the cashier is doing this, the bag boy hands each player a Bible. Players must not open the Bibles until cashier gives the signal. Cashier selects one of the Bible references handed him by the player and calls the book, chapter and number. At the sound of the bell, players open their Bible and find and read the verse. The first player to find and read the verse has won a point for his side. If player can quote verse from memory as soon as cashier calls out reference he has scored three points for his side. Then the cashier reads the second reference in the same manner. When the two verses have been found and read, cashier marks score for groups and players take their places at the foot of their lines where the bag boy has transfered their chairs from the front. The game continues with the next two players going to the market and so on. Cashier must be sure to score points and merchandise separately. When all players have had their turn shopping in the market, cashier totals score to find the group winner. Highest point score plus variety score decides the winner. Variety score is determined by group having a verse from every box or the one who comes the nearest to the variety. Example: A group may have four points which include only meat and bread and the other group may have four points which include meat, bread, clothing and milk. Of course this group would have high score on variety. This score counts five extra points which is added to the other points received in play. Variety score is not decided by the number of each but the most different kinds.

POP THE SECRET

Divide guests into two equal groups. Each group chooses a captain. Groups are seated across from each other. Players in one group have a discussion for a few minutes and decide on a secret. Secrets must be related to the New Testament. Example: One of our players can quote all of I Corinthians, chapter 13. Other secrets might be a player whose name is the same as someone mentioned in the Bible or someone in the group may have studied a particular lesson the previous Sunday in Sunday school. Any such thing may be a secret.

When the leader gives the signal the captain of the group with the secret starts the game by going to the other group to be questioned. This group tries to quiz him into revealing the secret of his group. The visiting captain can only answer by saying "Yes" or "No." Example: Question asked by the group may be as follows: "Does your secret have to do with a particular book of the New Testament?" Answer would be, "Yes." "Is it the book of John?" Answer would be, "No." Another question might be, "Does it have to do with memory work?" Answer would be, "Yes." "Is it a whole chapter?" Answer is "Yes, it is I Corinthians, chapter 13." In this instance the secret would be popped. Each member may ask four questions, two at a time. If the captain of the questioning group cannot "Pop the Secret" with questions, he must pass to the player next to him who will ask the next two and so on down the line.

If the secret is not popped by the last player the captain may ask two more questions and so on down the line until each player has asked four questions. If the questioning group is able to "Pop the Secret" they have scored fifty points and the visiting player must drop out of the game because he has not been able to keep a secret. If the group cannot "Pop the Secret" the visiting player returns to his group and another player is sent with another secret. Players may visit more than once but there must always be a new secret. Questions should be short and secrets should not be too detailed. Leader should keep score and give a prize to the group who pops the secret the greatest number of times within the period of play allowed. A large bag of popcorn for the group would be appropriate.

Relay Games

STAND UP, CHRISTIAN

Everyone knows how the early Christians were persecuted. Divide players into two equal groups. Each group must form a single line facing a goal. Each group must choose a captain who must sit on the floor at the head of his group about fifteen feet from the first player in his line. Players in the line also sit on the floor with legs crossed. When the leader blows the whistle the first player jumps up, runs forward, gets the captain by the hand and pulls him to his feet as he says, "Stand Up." The captain remains standing as first player runs back to the next in line, grabs player's hand and says, "Stand Up." Then first player takes his place at the foot of the line as second player goes forward and shakes the captain's hand. He then rushes back to the next in line and helps him up and so on down the line until all players are standing. First group to accomplish this is the winning group. Players must not rise from the floor until their hand is touched.

GOLD IN THE BANK

Divide guests into two equal groups. One group will be known as The Receivers and the other group as the The Givers. They may sit in two lines facing each other. Each group selects a manager. The leader acts as the banker and sits at a small table between the two groups. On the table is a Bible, a pencil and plain sheets of paper on which the banker will keep the number of points scored by each group. Banker has prepared in advance the accounts of each group. These accounts are the gold (Scripture verses) owned by each group. These accounts are different but there are the same number of verses in each account. Banker may choose as many verses as he wishes in making up the accounts, ten or more for each group. He will want to make them resemble actual bank statements. These accounts simply state the book in the New Testament, the chapter and verse number. An example is that the account of The Receivers, may have in it Romans 3:23, II Timothy 2:15, and so forth while the account of The Givers may have John 3:16, Revelation 3:20 etc. References should be equally distributed as to familiar and unfamiliar verses. When the banker hands the manager of The Giver group the statement of their account the game begins. The manager talks a few minutes with the players in his group, whispering to them about the gold in their account and they must decide on which verse they wish to give to The Receivers. When this is decided the manager writes a check (checks should be given out by the banker and resemble real checks) to The Receivers stating the name of the book, chapter number and verse number. Example: Pay to The Receivers John 3:16. Signed, The Givers. The manager of The Giver group hands the check to the manager of The Receivers. This group is allowed a few seconds to consult as to the answer. If anyone of the group knows the verse from memory he must take the check to the bank and get it cashed. Example: The player from The Receivers asks the banker to cash his check. The banker explains that he must first know what the check is for. If the player can quote the verse his check represents he has scored twenty-five points for his group. If he does not know it from memory but can tell it in his own words he scores fifteen points for his group. If the banker has to read the verse for the player the group receives five points if they can perform a feat which must be given to them by the banker. When the check is cashed player returns to his group and The Givers continue the game by writing another from their account. After a set number of verses have been given, the banker has the groups exchange places and The Receivers become The Givers. The banker must have the statement ready for this group. At the close of the contest the banker announces the winner which is the group scoring the highest number of points.

DUST THE TABLE

Dust the Table is a relay — Divide guests into two groups and have them stand in two single lines facing two tables which are the goals. Tables should be placed about twenty feet away, one at the head of each line. Place a chair beside the table and a Bible on the seat of each chair. Lay a dust cloth on the floor near each chair and across the back of each chair lay a folded tablecloth (a paper cloth may be used). At the sound of the leader's whistle the first player in each line must run to the table, pick up the dust cloth and wipe the entire table top. Then he must rush back and give the cloth to the player next in his group, who takes the cloth and runs to the table and dusts it in the same way and so on down the line until it reaches the last player in the line. The last player must not only dust the table, but after throwing the dust cloth on the floor, he must unfold the tablecloth, spread it on the table, take the Bible from the chair and place it on the table and then sit down in the chair. The group whose last player first accomplishes this is declared the winner.

OPEN THE BOOK

Leader asks players to count off one and two. Have all the ones form a group and the twos another group. Ask them to stand in two lines facing each other.

The leader gives first player in each line a pocket size New Testament and says, "When the whistle blows you are to open the Bible, find the verse of Scripture (leader gives same verse to both captains), read it aloud, close the Bible and hand it to the next in line and at the same time, ask him to find and read a verse of Scripture and so on down the line. When the person at the end of the line has read he must close the book and pass it back through the line to the first player or the captain." Leader should see that each player completes his verse. He will need to choose someone to help him. Players will be reading at the same time. The group whose captain receives the Bible first wins the contest. Leader might ask that verses from only one book be selected such as the book of John. Same verses may be used but not in succession. The player will naturally try to think of short verses. Care must also be exercised in handling the Bible.

LEAVEN IN THE MEAL

This is a Relay. Players are divided into two equal groups. Each group forms a line facing a goal about fifteen feet away. The goal is a table at the head of each line on which is placed a rather deep pan containing sand. The sand represents the meal. Leader will need to bury deep in the sand a marble for each player. These are the leaven. Cut a small hole in the top of a tiny box and give a box to the first player in each line. When the game begins the first player must rush to the table, dig out a marble, using only the left hand, drop it in the box, take it to the second player who runs to the table to find another marble and so on down the line. After player has had his turn he must go to the end of the line. The group that finishes first is the winner, providing they have the correct number of marbles in their box. If any player in either group spills the sand the game does not count and must be played again.

WALKING IN THE LIGHT

Choose sides for a relay. Have an equal number of players on each side. Have groups form two single lines facing a goal. At the end of each line, some distance from the first player, place a stack of cards. Cards should be about six inches square. There should be several more than a card for each player. Leader must have written on cards parts of Scripture verses that tell how to "walk in the light." There must be at least one of these or more for each player. Other cards will have verses that do not relate to walking in the light but rather walking in darkness. Example: A card may have "walk in steps of faith" while another may have "walk in hate." Place cards on the floor in a jumbled manner, printed side up. When the leader gives the signal, first player must walk to the pile of cards, select a card with appropriate Scripture verse on how to walk, take it to the other end of the room and lean it against the wall with the printed side out. Then he must walk back to the second player in his line and shake his hand and then take his place at the foot of the line. The second player must start walking as soon as player shakes his hand. Player proceeds to cards, selects one and leans it against the wall with the other and so on down the line. When the last player in the line has had his turn and is back in line, players shout, "We are walking in the light." First group to shout is the winner. Leader must check cards selected by each group. If there are those that do not tell the correct way to walk, that group is disqualified.

Some verses on how to walk in the light are:

Walk uprightly, walk and not faint, walk the good way, walk humbly, walk in faith, walk in brightness, walk in the commandments, walk in grace, walk in integrity, walk with God, walk in His teachings, walk in the law and walk in truth.

Some verses on how not to walk are:

Walk in pride, walk in selfishness, walk in envy, walk in jealousy, walk in ways of the flesh, walk in darkness, walk disorderly, walk in craftiness.

FLASHLIGHT RELAY

This game is based on the stoy of the ten virgins having to do with the ones who were unprepared and had no oil for their lamps. In this relay, players do not have batteries in their flashlights. Divide players into two equal groups and have them line up facing a goal about fifteen feet away. A flashlight without batteries is placed on the chair at the head of each line. The leader gives the first player and the end player in each line a flashlight battery. When the leader gives the signal the first player must start his battery down the line by passing it with his left hand over his left shoulder while the end player must start his battery up the line by passing it with the right hand over the right shoulder of player in front of him. Batteries must be kept going and players are not allowed to hold them unless a player has received both batteries at the same time, one in his right hand and the other in his left. The first player to get both batteries must run to the chair, pick up flashlight, sit down in the chair and place in batteries. The group whose player is first to assemble and shine the flashlight is declared the winner. Batteries may have to be passed more than once. When making preparations leader should test batteries and flashlights to make sure they are in perfect working condition.

REMEMBER THE NAME RELAY

Write names, selected from the New Testament (apostles or others), on small cards (index cards will do), one name to each card. Divide players into two groups with the same number of players in each group. The groups should stand in lines facing each other, about six feet apart. Place a card on the floor in front of each player with names turned up. Players must remember the name on the card in front of them. Select two players to stand at the foot of each line. Give each of these players a small box. The leader should stand at the head of the lines. When the signal is given, the first player in each group must pick up the card in front of him and hand it to the player next to him, who must pick up the card in front of him and give both cards to the third player and so on down the line. Players must not pick up their card until they have been given the cards from the other player. The last player has all the cards which he must put in the box held by the player at the end of his line. This player must rush to the first player and hand him the box. First player must take all the cards out of the box and pass them down the line except his card which he keeps. Each player must keep his original card and pass the remainder to the next and so on until all players have the cards with which he started. Players must place card on the floor in front of them. The first group to assume the original position wins the relay. Leader will want to write down the names given each player.

One Word Games

MELT THE ICE

Melt the ice by finding the appropriate words ending in ice which fit the description of the sentence. Leader may read sentences or prepare copies in advance. Omit answers which are in parenthesis.

1. An ice every Christian should be. (nice)
2. An ice that gives a reward or penalty as deserved. (justice)
3. An ice who was the mother of Timothy. (Eunice)
4. Ices used by Satan. (devices)
5. An ice the chief priests declared to be of blood. (price)
6. An ice of divine ordinance. (service)
7. An ice which God requires of our bodies. (sacrifice)
8. An ice Christians should do in the glory of God. (rejoice)
9. An ice all Christians should lay aside. (malice)
10. An ice that Paul gave to the Corinthians. (advice)
11. An ice of fragrance or aroma. (spice)
12. An ice that seeks pleasure. (entice)
13. An ice that cuts into parts. (slice)
14. An ice that is food. (rice)
15. An ice Paul did not have in which to mail his letters. (post office)
16. An ice that is used when partaking of the Lord's Supper. (juice)
17. An ice that is evil. (vice)
18. An ice that is the number of times Peter denied Christ. (thrice)

PARTS OF A TESTAMENT

The Book

1. When one departs. (leaves)
2. The power of self control. (will)
3. Single line of poetry. (verse)
4. A division of a fraternity. (chapter)

5. To put on a coat. (cover)
6. The forefinger. (index)
7. A cloth with a design. (print)
8. Documents proving identity. (paper)
9. To plan in detail. (map)
10. A claim to a car. (title)
11. An agreement. (concordance)
12. A writing. (Scripture)
13. Likeness of persons or scenes. (pictures)

CONVERT THE CON

Players are given copies of the following sentences and asked to supply the answer with a word in which *con* appears. Leader should not allow over ten minutes answering time. Players may correct their paper as leader gives answers. A package of construction paper is an appropriate prize for the winner and a pine cone, sprayed with color, might be given the losing player as a consolation prize. Answers are in parenthesis.

1. A con that is happy. (*con*tent)
2. A con that makes us strong. (*con*fidence)
3. A con that changes us. (*con*vert)
4. A con that makes us feel guilty. (*con*science)
5. A con that can save our soul. (*con*fess)
6. A con interested in others. (*con*cern)
7. A con describing actions. (*con*duct)
8. A con in a house. (*con*crete)
9. A con expressing vanity. (*con*ceit)
10. A con accusing others. (*con*demn)
11. A con that fights. (*con*flict)
12. A con that agrees. (*con*form)
13. A con that understands. (*con*ceive)
14. A con that holds together. (*con*sist)
15. A con that devours. (*con*sume)
16. A con that seeks advice. (*con*sult)
17. A con that denies. (*con*tradict)
18. A con that overcomes. (*con*vince)
19. A con that is opposed. (*con*trary)
20. A con found in the Bible. (*con*cordance)

MINERAL, METAL OR STONE

Guests are given paper on which the following questions are typed or written. The answer is one word. It is one of the three —mineral, metal or stone.

1. What swings at an entrance? (agate)
2. What gets beneath the tissue and is painful? (carbuncle)
3. What word is slang for a hat worn by a staff officer in the army? (brass)
4. What is a thing every person will sometime have? (beryl)
5. What is one part of a woman's hat and the other part of a house? (brimstone)
6. What sticks to our shoes when wet? (clay)
7. What is a slang name given a law officer? (copper)
8. What is the infield called in baseball? (diamond)
9. Something that presses. (iron)
10. What is the thing in which food is preserved? (tin)
11. Something most every housewife needs a set of. (silver)
12. What is a game in which a thing is propelled by the thumb to hit another thing? (marble)
13. What is a part of a pencil? (lead)
14. Bits of dust that we wouldn't mind having around. (gold)
15. A thing that spins plus the first and last letter of the alphabet. (topaz)
16. A masculine name. (Jasper)
17. Something a boy usually says to girls in parting after a date. (nitre)

TRANSLATION

Leader should prepare in advance typewritten copies of the following and explain to guests that the Hebrew words in italics are names of the months. Have them identfy them by the clues given in each sentence. Omit answers in parenthesis.

1. The second letter of the Hebrew month *Nisan* is next to the last letter of our month which it represents. (April)
2. The third letter of *Lyar* is the middle letter in a three letter word. (May)

3. The last letter of *Sivan* is the third letter in a four letter word. (June)
4. Next to the last letter of *Tammuz* is the second letter in a four letter word. (July)
5. The first letter of *Ab* is the first letter in a six letter word. (August)
6. The first letter of *Elul* is the second letter in a nine letter word. (September)
7. The second letter of *Ethanim* is the third letter. (October)
8. The last letter of *Marchesvan* is the first letter. (November)
9. The first letter of *Chislev* is the third letter. (December)
10. None of the letters of *Tebeth* are in our month. (January)
11. The fourth letter of *Shebet* is the third letter. (February)
12. The first letter of Adar is the second in a five letter word. (March)

SEEK A WORD

Give each guest a slip of paper with the word *testament* printed at the top and the following sentences, omitting answers. The answers will be one word formed from letters in the word testament. Letters are not used twice unless they appear in the word twice.

1. What does a teacher give in school? (test)
2. What do boys sleep in when camping? (tent)
3. How is a female bird related to a male? (mate)
4. What are the tiny insects that sometimes get in our homes? (ants)
5. Something we do three times a day. (eat)
6. Groups that compete in contests. (teams)
7. A kind of food. (meat)
8. A part of a flower. (stem)
9. Name given to young people. (teen)
10. A thing used in catching fish. (net)
11. A word at the close of a prayer. (Amen)
12. Something placed at the front door. (mat)

13. Something we get at the beach. (tan)
14. Something sewn in a garment. (seam)
15. Something found in a tree. (nest)
16. A boy's name. (Sam)
17. A girl's hat. (tam)
18. Something good to drink. (tea)
19. Something a horse has. (mane)
20. The way one should always look in his appearance. (neat)

INVISIBLE WORD

Give each player a pencil and paper on which the following sentences have been copied. Ask them to find one word in answer to each sentence. Answers are in parenthesis. A suitable prize would be a tiny dictionary.

1. The part of a band instrument is something the rich are likely to fall into. (snare — drum)
2. The wife of Ananias is the name of a precious stone. (sapphire)
3. A part of our hand is a tree that was familiar in Palestine. (palm)
4. A gem mentioned in Revelation is the name of a small fish. (sardine)
5. One of our heavenly bodies is the title of Christ in Revelation. (Morning Star)
6. Things used in corsets were carried by the multitudes led by Judas. (staves)
7. The name used to describe a natural ability is the thing Jesus gave to the servants. (talent)
8. The part of our income after certain deductions is what Jesus saw James and John mending. (net)
9. A shade of green is the name of a mountain which Jesus visited often. (Olive)
10. The name of a boy was used in building houses. (Clay)
11. The thing that decorates a woman's hat is the part of the temple that was rent at the crucifixion. (veil)
12. A part of an egg is the thing Peter asked the people not to put upon the neck of the disciples. (yoke)

13. The thing in which we cook our food is the name Jesus used when He referred to Paul as chosen. (vessel)
14. That which is done through a legal process to take a child into a family is the title given the Holy Spirit in Romans, chapter 8. (adoption)
15. A seasoning used in food is what Jesus applied to the disciples of the earth. (salt)
16. The thing we do to a friend in sorrow is a title of the Holy Spirit. (Comfort-er)
17. Something we do to certain people running for office is a title applied to Christians. (Elect)
18. Something we buy in a pair is what the Lord asked Moses to remove when standing on holy ground. (shoes)
19. A kind of tablecloth is the material of the clothing worn by the angels when they came out of the Temple. (linen)
20. A place where every young girl hopes to walk to is where we place our offerings. (altar)

DESCRIPTION

Name as many persons, places or things (mentioned in the New Testament) that the word *Holy* is used to describe. Answers must be one word.

Some are listed:

Holy Scripture	Holy Jerusalem	Holy Spirit
Holy Commandment	Holy City	Holy Body
Holy Temple	Holy Sabbath	Holy House
Holy Ghost	Holy Nation	Holy Angels
Holy Brethren	Holy Day	Holy Father
Holy Hands	Holy Man	Holy Child
Holy Bishop	Holy Heaven	Holy Mount
Holy Priest		